World Book's Learning Ladders

Animal Babies

WORLD
BOOK

a Scott Fetzer company
Chicago
www.worldbookonline.com

WORLD BOOK

233 N. Michigan Avenue
Chicago, IL 60601
U.S.A.

For information about other World Book publications, visit our Web site at
http://www.worldbookonline.com or call **1-800-WORLDBK (967-5325).**

For information about sales to schools and libraries, call **1-800-975-3250 (United States);**
1-800-837-5365 (Canada).

Library of Congress Cataloging-in-Publication Data

Animal babies.
    p. cm. -- (World Book's learning ladders)
  Includes index.
    Summary: "Introduction to animal babies using simple
text, illustrations, and photos. Features include puzzles
and games, fun facts, a resource list, and an index"--
Provided by publisher.
  ISBN 978-0-7166-7736-9
    1. Animals--Infancy--Juvenile literature. I. World Book,
Inc.
  QL763.A533 2011
  591.3'9--dc22
                                        2010022382

World Book's Learning Ladders
Set 2 ISBN: 978-0-7166-7746-8

Printed in China by Shenzhen Wing King Tong Paper Products Co., Ltd.
Shenzhen, Guangdong
1st printing December 2010

Editorial
  Editor in Chief: Paul A. Kobasa
  Associate Manager, Supplementary Publications:
    Cassie Mayer
  Writer: Shawn Brennan
  Editor: Brian Johnson
  Researcher: Cheryl Graham
  Manager, Contracts & Compliance
  (Rights & Permissions): Loranne K. Shields

Graphics and Design
  Manager: Tom Evans
  Coordinator, Design Development and Production:
    Brenda B. Tropinski
  Photographs Editor: Kathy Creech

Pre-Press and Manufacturing
  Director: Carma Fazio
  Manufacturing Manager: Steven Hueppchen
  Production/Technology Manager: Anne Fritzinger

Photographic credits: Cover: © Westend61/SuperStock; WORLD BOOK illustration by Q2A Media;
Shutterstock; p4, p6, p8, p11: Getty Images; p12, p22, p26, p27, p28, p29: Shutterstock;
p17, p18, p20: Alamy Images.

Illustrators: WORLD BOOK illustration by Q2A Media

What's inside?

This book tells you about the different ways that animal babies live, learn, and grow. Some babies look just like their parents and others look very different.

Bear

It's springtime and two black bear cubs are ready to play! They spent the long winter in a den with their mother, drinking her milk while she slept. Now the mother will teach them to hunt for food.

A mother polar bear lives with her cubs in a den. She digs her den in a snowbank on the side of a hill.

Cubs like to play. This helps them to learn about hunting.

Strong **jaws** are good for catching fish.

Thick **fur** keeps the bears warm during the cold winter.

It's a fact!

The phrase "licked into shape" comes from an old belief that bears were born so soft and shapeless that their mothers had to lick them into their shape.

Black bear cubs have long, sharp **claws**, just like their mother. They use their claws to climb trees and to hunt.

5

Opossum

Last spring, a mother opossum *(uh POS uhm)* gave birth to a litter of babies, called kits. The tiny babies lived for many weeks inside a pouch on their mother's belly. They drank her milk and grew bigger. Now they are ready to leave the mother's pouch. They will ride on her back until they are able to walk on their own!

A possum is an animal related to opossums. It lives in Australia, New Guinea, and nearby islands.

Opossums have **feet** that work like hands to grasp things.

Young opossum **kits** travel by riding on their mother's back.

It's a fact!
A newborn opossum is about as big as a kidney bean!

A long, hairless **tail** is good for climbing trees and hanging upside down!

7

Frog

A mother frog has just laid her eggs in a pond. In a few days, tiny animals called tadpoles will hatch from the eggs. The tadpoles will stay in the water as they grow. They will go through many changes before they become adult frogs!

Some male frogs make good fathers. This male frog protects his eggs until they hatch.

Frogs begin life inside an **egg.**

Tadpoles are born with **tails** that are shaped like paddles for swimming.

Young tadpoles have **gills** for breathing underwater.

Tadpoles begin to grow **hind legs.**

The tail disappears into the body.

Lungs develop and replace the gills. Now the frog can breathe air outside the water.

Then **front legs** begin to grow.

9

Fish

A female salmon has finished a long journey upstream. She has returned to the place where she was born to mate and lay eggs. The female digs a nest with her tail to protect her eggs. When the baby salmon hatch, they stay in the nest as their bodies change and grow. Then the young salmon will travel back down the river to the ocean!

It's a fact!

Some fish carry their eggs in their mouth!

Salmon begin life inside an **egg.**

Baby salmon have a **yolk sac** attached to their bodies. The yolk sac contains food.

A seahorse is a fish with a head that looks like the head of a horse. A female seahorse lays her eggs in a pouch on the male's belly. After the eggs hatch, the male releases the tiny young.

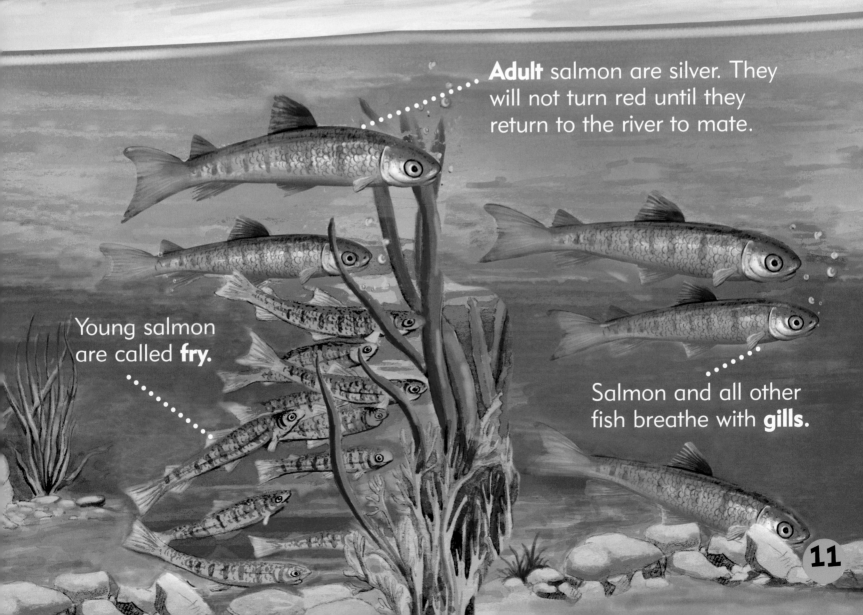

Adult salmon are silver. They will not turn red until they return to the river to mate.

Young salmon are called **fry.**

Salmon and all other fish breathe with **gills.**

Insect

It is summer in North America. A noisy bug called a cicada has returned to the trees where it was born. The cicada lived underground for years as its body grew and changed. It came out of the ground as a winged adult, ready to make some noise!

It's a fact!

Carpenter bees lay the largest eggs of all insects.

1

2

The young cicadas **hatch** from the eggs. Then they drop to the ground and crawl into the earth.

A monarch caterpillar goes through many changes before it becomes a beautiful butterfly.

6 The winged **adult** is ready to mate.

A female adult lays her **egg**s in a tree branch.

5 The cicada sheds its **skin**.

4 When a cicada grows big enough, it crawls out of the ground.

3 Cicadas live **underground** for years. They suck juice from tree roots.

Babes in the woods

It's a lovely spring day and lots of animal babies are exploring. What kinds of animal babies do you see?

Which animals have gills?

14

Words you know

Here are some words that you learned earlier. Say them out loud, then try to find the things in the picture.

cub   kit   tadpole
claws   gills   caterpillar

Which baby is crawling on a tree branch?

Kangaroo

A baby kangaroo is getting ready to leave the pouch on its mother's belly. It spent many months there drinking its mother's milk and growing. But the baby kangaroo is not yet ready to live on its own. It will stay close to its mother for many months to learn how to be a grown-up!

A baby kangaroo is called a **joey**. A joey lives in a **pouch** on the mother's belly.

Small **front legs** are used to dig and pull leaves off trees to eat.

A kangaroo hops on its large, powerful **hind legs**.

It's a fact!

A newborn kangaroo could fit into a teaspoon!

A kangaroo has long, narrow **feet**.

A kangaroo can turn its large **ears** from front to back.

A koala baby is also called a joey. The joey lives in its mother's pouch for seven months. Then it rides on her back for the next six months.

A kangaroo uses its big, long **tail** for balance and pushing off.

Bird

Most birds build nests to lay eggs, but not the emperor penguin! A mother emperor penguin lays an egg. Then she goes away for weeks to get food. The father holds the egg on top of his feet. He keeps it warm under the fluffy, feathered fold of his belly. After the egg hatches, the father keeps the chick safe and warm in this cozy "nest" until the mother returns.

Thick layers of **fat** keep the penguin's body warm.

Another good daddy bird is the emu *(EE myoo)*, a large Australian bird that cannot fly. The father sits on the eggs until they hatch.

A penguin chick stays warm under the fold of its father's belly.

It's a
fact!
Some birds keep
their eggs warm
by burying them
near volcanoes!

Waterproof **feathers** ......
keep the penguin's
body dry and warm.

A penguin has **wings** like
flippers. These help the
penguin to swim.

As a chick grows, its
fluffy down is replaced
by adult feathers.

 # Platypus

The platypus *(PLAT uh puhs)* is a strange creature that lives along streams in Australia. It has a snout like a duck's beak. It also has webbed feet and thick, brown fur. When a female is ready to lay eggs, she builds a nest underground. She keeps her eggs safe and warm on her belly. After the babies hatch, they stay in the nest. They feed on their mother's milk and grow.

The platypus has a coat of thick **fur.**

The echidna *(ih KIHD nuh)* is another strange Australian animal that lays eggs and feeds its babies milk. This picture shows a baby echidna.

A broad, flat **tail** works like a paddle for swimming.

Webbed feet help the platypus swim.

The platypus uses its **bill** to scoop up worms and shellfish from the bottom of streams.

Sharp **claws** help the platypus dig burrows.

It's a fact!

Scientists believe platypuses lived during the time of the dinosaurs!

Lizard

The bearded dragon is a kind of lizard that lives in Australia. It has a spiny pouch of skin around its neck that looks like a beard. The lizard puffs out the pouch when it wants to look scary. When a mother bearded dragon is ready to lay eggs, she digs a hole for a nest. When the babies hatch, they look and act just like their parents, only smaller!

It's a fact!

In Central America, iguanas (a kind of lizard) are sometimes called "chicken of the trees." This is because many people like to eat them!

what's for dinner?

The Komodo dragon is the largest lizard in the world. It weighs more than an adult person!

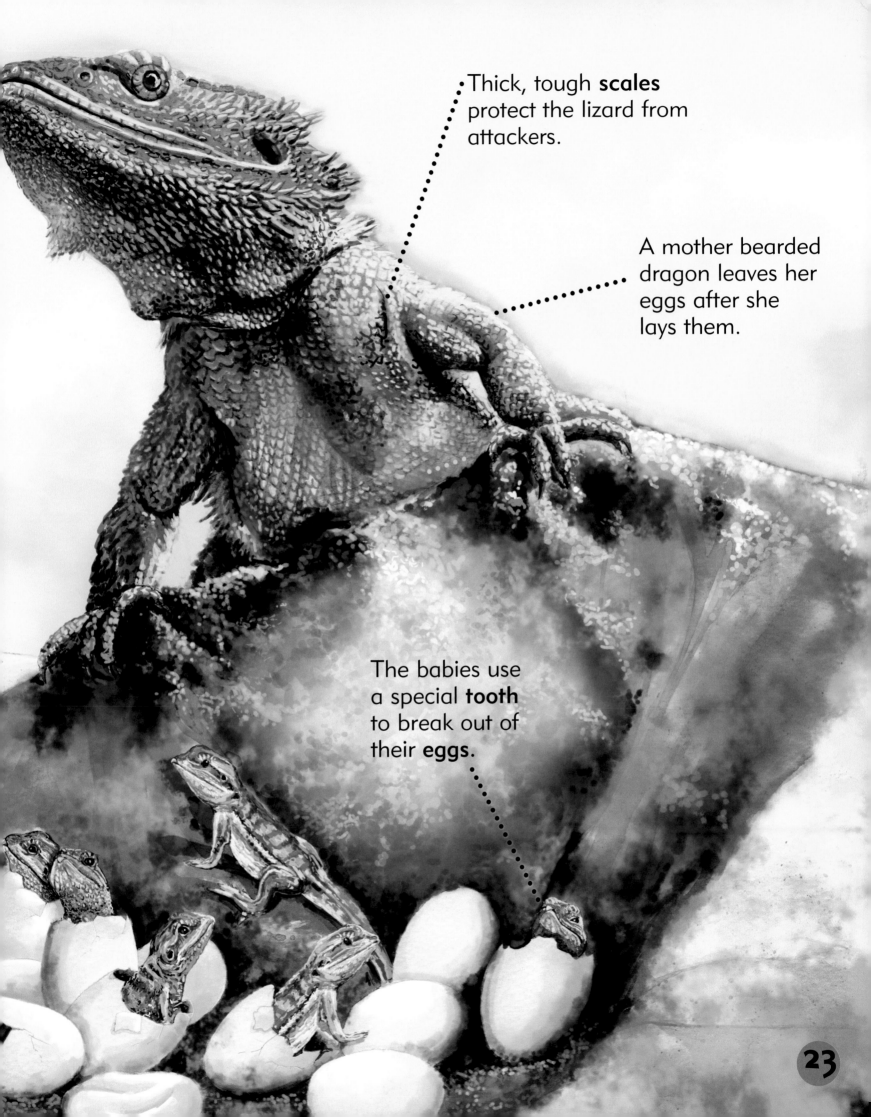

Thick, tough **scales** protect the lizard from attackers.

A mother bearded dragon leaves her eggs after she lays them.

The babies use a special **tooth** to break out of their **eggs**.

Babes in the outback

The outback is a wild and beautiful area of Australia. Can you find some of the outback babies you have met in this book?

24

Words you know

Here are some words that you learned earlier. Say them out loud, then try to find the things in the picture.

feathers   joey   scales
eggs   pouch   tail

How many baby lizards are hatching?

Did you know?

Crocodiles lay eggs. When the babies are ready to hatch, they send grunting messages to their mother. She then cracks the shells with her teeth!

Pup, the name for a baby dog, is also the name for a baby bat, hamster, seal, shark, squirrel, walrus, and many other animals.

Pup

A joey that has left its mother's pouch but still returns to nurse is called a "young-at-foot."

Some male frogs swallow their mate's eggs and keep them safe in a mouth pouch! The babies hatch and stay in the pouch until they grow into adult frogs.

Female giraffes give birth to their babies standing up. Because the mother is so tall, its newborn drops down 5 feet (1.5 meters) or more onto the ground!

Puzzles

Close-up!

We've zoomed in on three animal babies. Can you figure out which animal babies you are looking at?

1

2

3

Answers on page 32.

When I grow up...

What will each baby look like when it grows up? Follow the lines to find out!

tadpole   cub   caterpillar

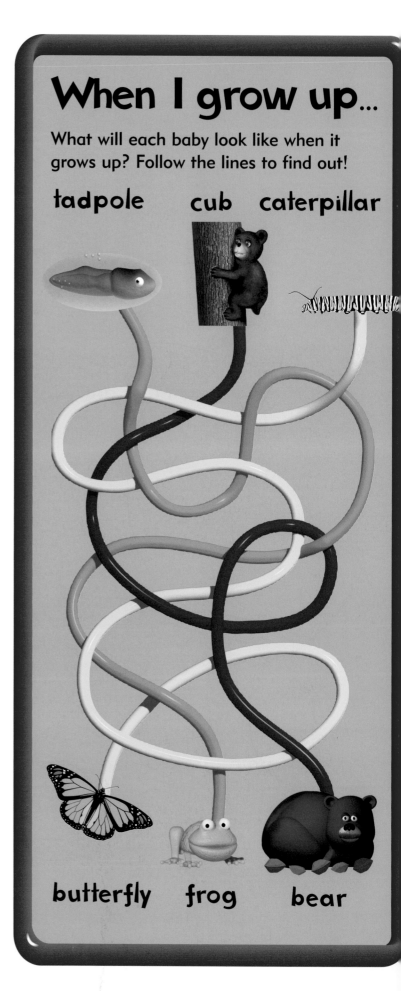

butterfly   frog   bear

Who's alike?

1 Which 6 babies hatch from eggs?

2 Which 4 babies drink their mother's milk?

3 Which 3 babies live inside their parent's pouch?

opossum kit

tadpole

bear cub

lizard

penguin chick

cicada

kangaroo joey

seahorse

platypus

29

Answers on page 32.

True or false

Can you figure out which of these statements are true? Turn to the page numbers given to help you find the answers.

A newborn opossum is about as big as a kidney bean.
Go to page 7.

3

Platypuses lived during the time of the dinosaurs.
Go to page 21.

1

what's for dinner?

4

In Central America, iguanas are sometimes called "dog of the land."
Go to page 22.

2

Tadpoles can grow up to 10 feet (3 meters) long.
Go to page 9.

5

Cicadas lay the largest eggs of all insects.
Go to page 12.

Answers on page 32.

Find out more

Books

Animal Babies (Kingfisher, 2005-2007). Ten volumes: *…Around the House, … in Deserts, … in Grasslands, … in Polar Lands, … in Ponds and Rivers, … in Rain Forests, … in Seas, … in Towns and Cities, … on Mountains, … on the Farm.*
Learn about animal babies in all kinds of environments.

Animal Families by Lorrie Mack (Dorling Kindersley, 2008)
Some kinds of animals have family relationships. You can learn about them in this book.

Carry Me! Animal Babies on the Move by Susan Stockdale (Peachtree Publishers, 2005)
Animals around the world have many ways of transporting their young, and this book tells how they do it.

How Do Animal Babies Live? by Faith Hickman Brynie (Enslow Publishers, 2010)
Find out how different animals take care of their babies and what happens to the babies as they grow up.

How Many Baby Pandas? by Sandra Markle (Walker & Company, 2009)
Follow eight panda pairs as they live and grow at China's Wolong Giant Panda Breeding and Research Center.

Some Babies Are Wild by Marion Dane Bauer and Stan Tekiela (Adventure Publications, 2008)
Learn about the relationships between wild baby animals and their mothers.

Web sites

Baby Animals Guide
http://animal.discovery.com/guides/baby-animals/baby-animals.html
Choose from a list of birds, mammals, insects, and reptiles for a photograph and short description of the baby animal.

Photo Gallery: Baby Animals
http://animals.nationalgeographic.com/animals/photos/baby-animals.html
National Geographic's picture collection of baby animals.

Word List: Animals and Their Young
http://www.abcteach.com/free/l/list_animals_and_young.pdf
A list of nearly 50 animals, with the names used for their babies.

ZooBorns
http://www.zooborns.com/
Photographs of baby animals born in zoos and aquariums.

Answers

Puzzles
from pages 28 and 29

Close-up!
1. kangaroo joey
2. penguin chick
3. tadpole

Who's alike?
1. cicada, lizard, penguin chick, platypus, seahorse, tadpole
2. bear cub, kangaroo joey, opossum kit, platypus
3. kangaroo joey, opossum kit, seahorse egg

True or false
from page 30

1. true
2. false
3. true
4. false
5. false

Index